EUROPEAN FLAVOR II

MB99928

BY JAMES C. FAZIO

Table of Contents

An Old French Town

James C. Fazio

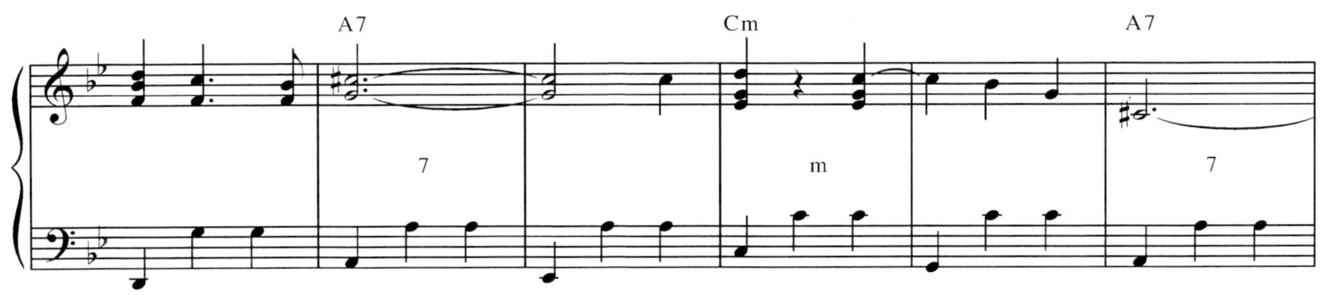

Cm
A7
m
7
D7
G7
Cm
7
7
m
F7
Bb
D7
Gm
7
M
7
m
A7
7
Cm
Gm
D7
Gm
m
m
7
1.
m

Gm
F7
Bb
D7
2.
m
7
M
7
Gm
Cm
D7
m
m
7
Bb
Eb
Cm
D7
Gm
M
M
m
7
m
A7
To Coda
Cm
7
Coda
Cm
Gm
D7
Gm
m
m
7
m

Volkmarch Polka

James C. Fazio

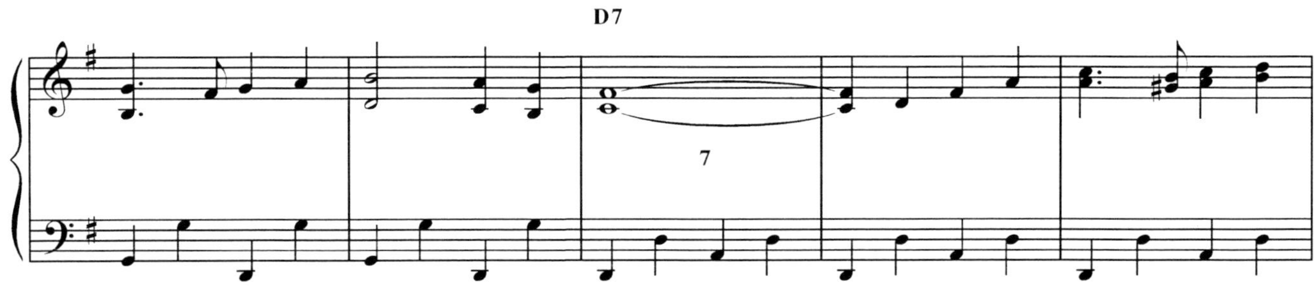

C
M
Bass solo
G
D7
G
1.
M
7
M
Bass solo
G
2.
C
M
Bass solo
M
M
G7
7

C
Bass solo
M
C7
7
F
M
C
M
G7
7
C
1.
M
Bass solo
C
2.
M
Bass solo
F
M
C7
7
F
M

Dance of the Matador

James C. Fazio

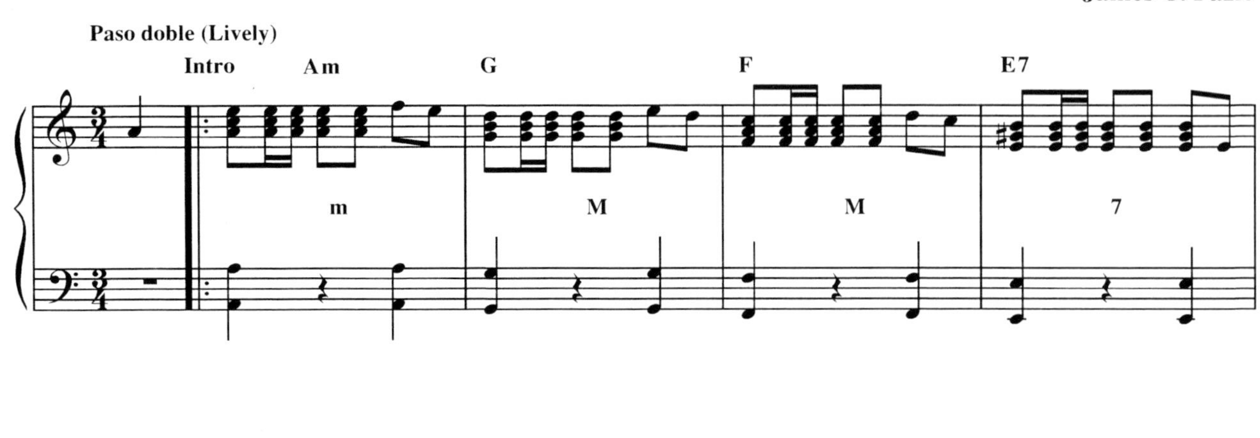

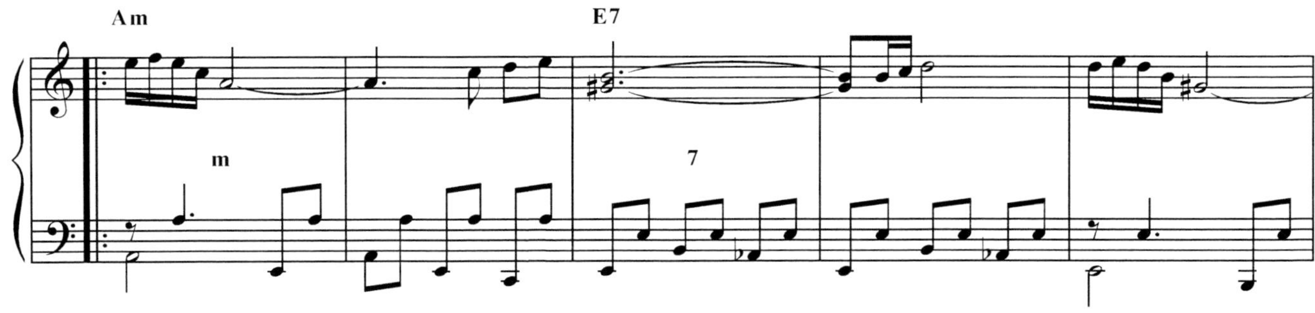

G
F
E7
1.
M
M
7
E7
2.
C
M
G
C
M
M
E7
Am
7
m
3
G
F
E7
F
E7
1.
E7
2.
M
M
7
M
7
solo
7

Am
F
M
C7
7
M
F
Bb
F
D7
M
7
G7
C
Gm
1.
2.
7
M
m
F
F#
F
7
M
M
M

Una Festa

James C. Fazio

Dm
A7
m
7
Dm
D
1.
2.
m
M
A7
7
D
M

G
M
D
A7
M
7
D
1.
M
D
2.
bass solo
G
M
D7
7

G
M
G7
7
C
Cm
G
M
m
M
D7
G
G
7
1.
M
2.
M

Loire Tango

James C. Fazio

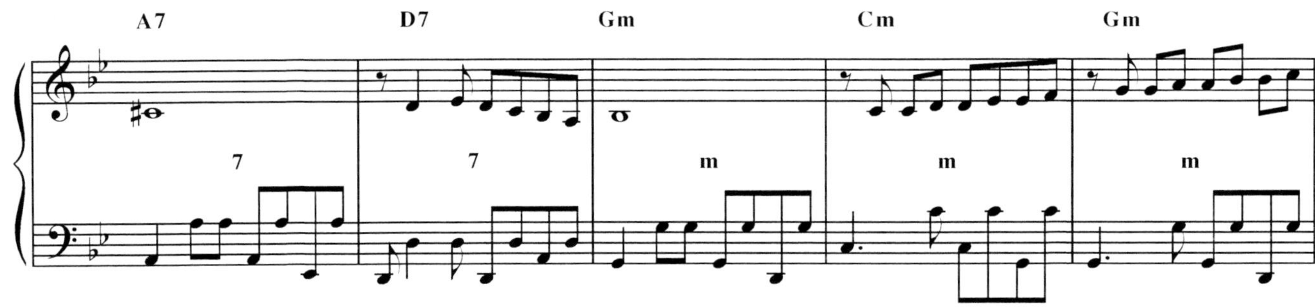

Gm
A7
D7
Gm
m
7
7
m
Cm
Gm
A7
D7
m
m
7
7
Gm
A7
D7
Gm
m
7
7
m
Cm
Gm
D7
Gm
m
m
7
m
F7
Bb
D7
Gm
7
M
7
m

La Tristezza Gira Alla Gioia

(Sadness Turns to Joy)

James C. Fazio

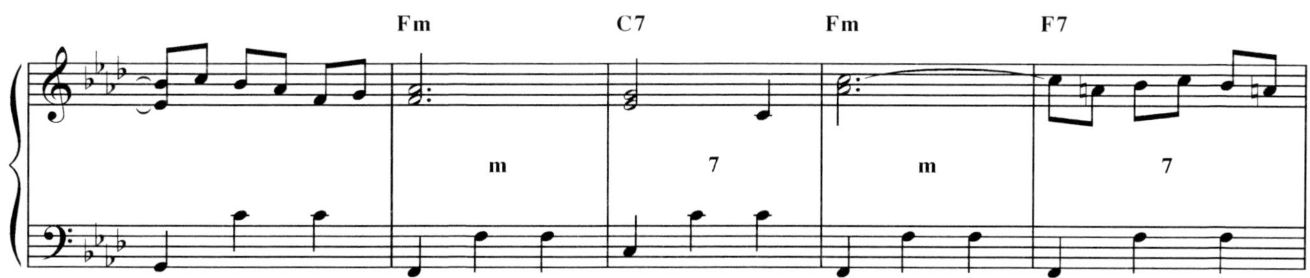

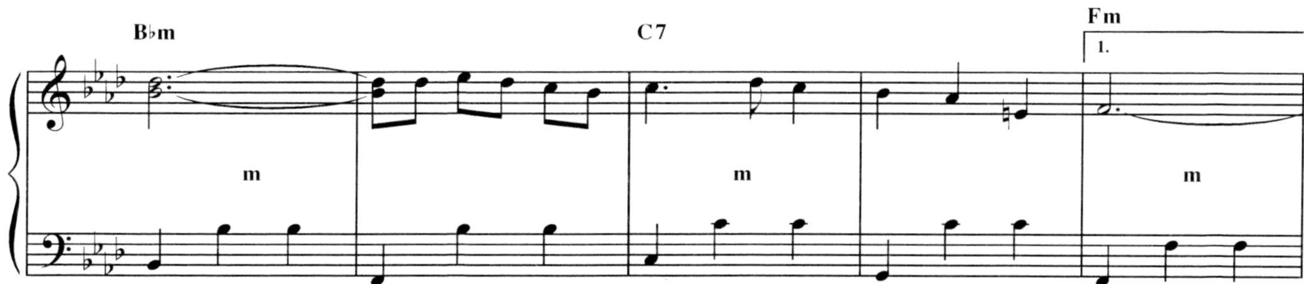

23

Fm
Bbm
Eb7
m
m
7
Ab
Db
C7
Fm
M
M
m
F7
Bbm
Eb7
Ab
Db
7
m
7
M
M
C7
Fm
F
7
1.
2.
m
m
F
Gm
C7
M
m
7

F
C 7
F
Gm
A 7
m
7
Dm
B♭
F
m
M
M
C 7
7
F
1.
M
F
2.
M
Bass solo
7
M
M
M

Strasbourg Waltz

James C. Fazio

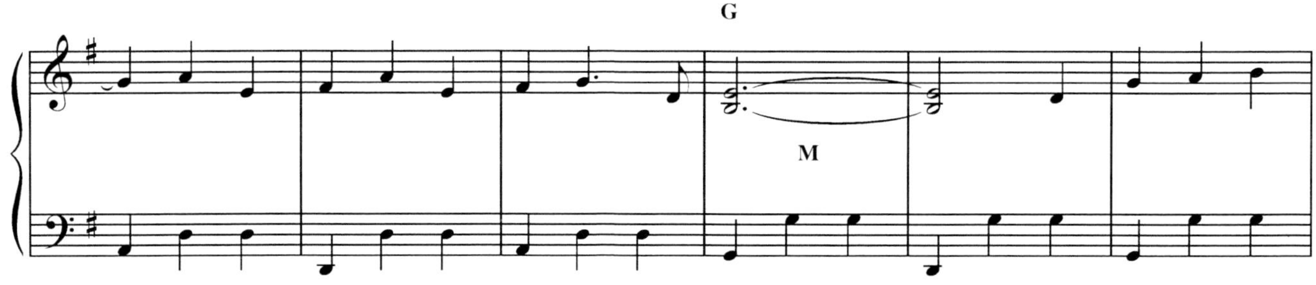

Am
G
D7
m
M
7
G
G
D7
1.
2.
M
M
7
Solo
Solo
G
D7
G
M
7
M
D7
G
D7
7
M
7
G
G
G7
C
1.
2.
M
M
7
M
Solo
Solo

Die Alpen Joddler

James C. Fazio

C7
7
F
M
F7
7
B♭
M
F
M

C7
F
1.
7
M
solo
F
2.
G7
C
M
7
M
G7
C
7
M
G7
C
G
7
M
7
C
1.
C
2.
M
M

Dance of the Gypsies

James C. Fazio

E7
Am
E7
Bass solo
A7
Dm
G7
C
E7
1.
E7
2.
Am
E7
Am
E7

Bordeaux Waltz

James C. Fazio

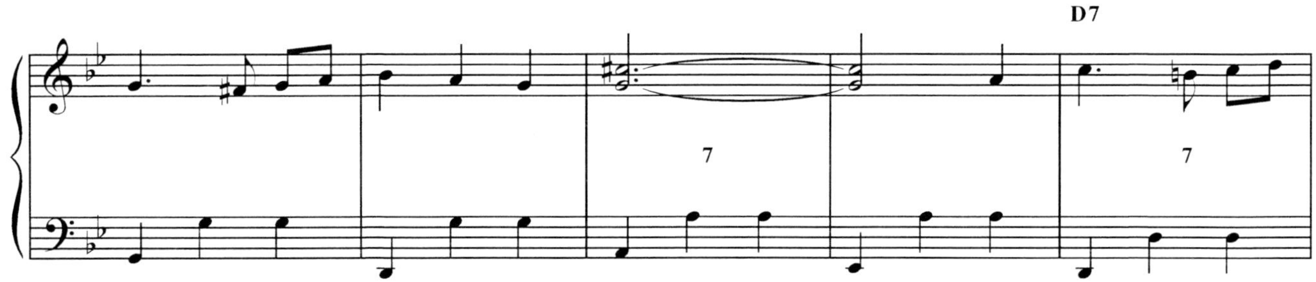

G7
Cm
F7
B♭
E♭
A7
1.
D7
D7
2.
Gm
F7
B♭
D7
Gm
Cm

G
M
D7
7
G
M
D7
7
B7
7
E7
Am
m
D7
7
G
1.
M
G
2.
M

Die Rhineland Polka

James C. Fazio

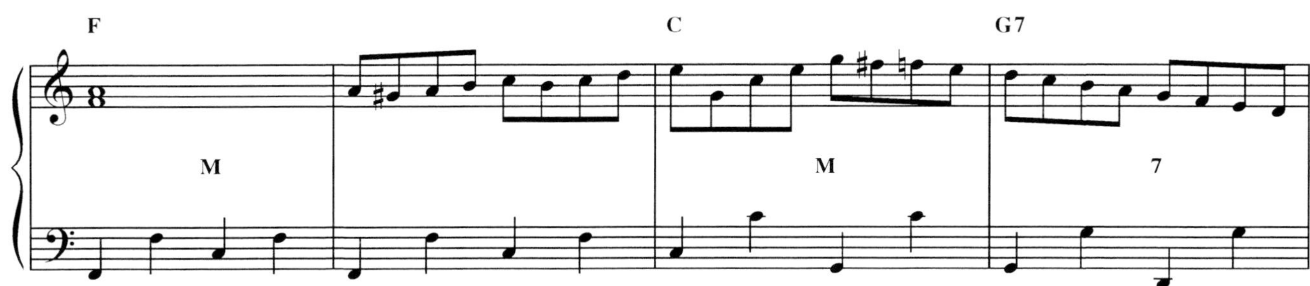

Morning in Paris

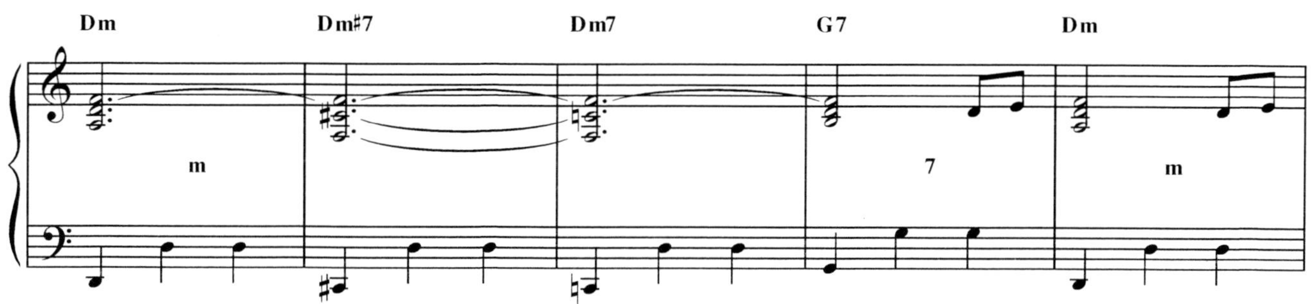

Dm
G7
A7
D7
m
7
7
7
G
Am
D7
G
M
m
7
M
G7
C
Cm7
C6
B♭dim
Dm
7
M
dim.
m
Dm♯7
Dm7
G7
Dm
Dm♯7
Dm7
7
m
G7
C
A7
Dm
M
7
m

Fm
C
A7
bass solo
m
M
7
C
A7
Dm
G7
To Coda
bass solo
M
7
m
7
C
D7
G
B7
M
7
M
7
Em
Am
B7
m
m
7
G
C
Am
B7
Coda
M
M
m
7

Il Nonno
(Grandfather)

James C. Fazio

Gm
Dm
m
m
A7
Dm
1.
7
m
D
D
A7
2.
M
7
D
M
A7
7

D
M
A7
7
B7
7
Em
m
D
M
A7
D
1.
M
D
2.
M
G
M

Italian Nights

James C. Fazio

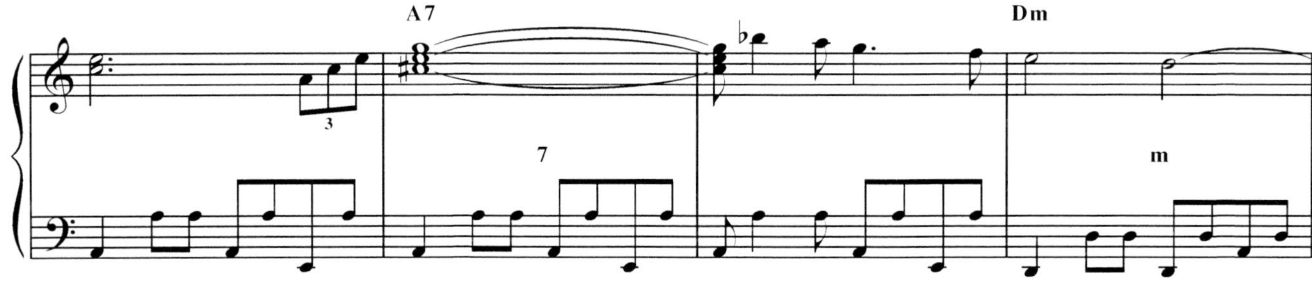

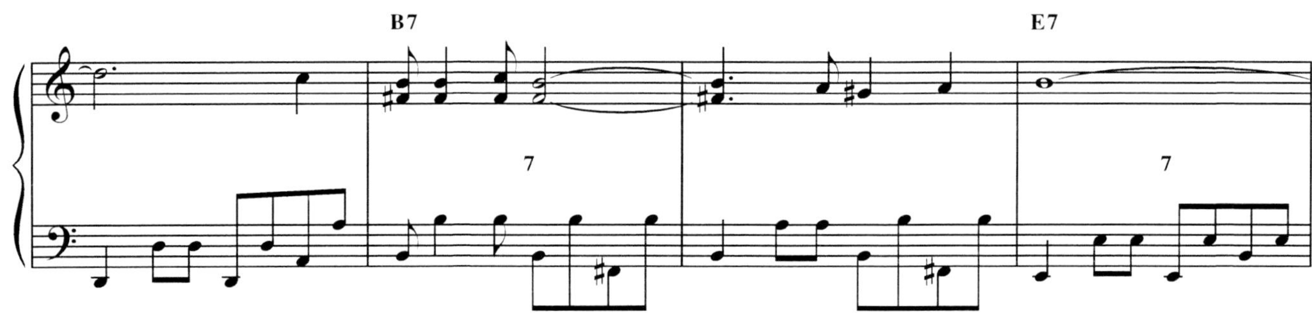

MEL BAY PUBLICATIONS, INC. • www.MELBAY.com

UNIQUELY INTERESTING MUSIC!